Mirrors
for
Men

A Journal for Reflection

Justin O'Brien, Ph.D.

Yes International Publishers
Saint Paul, Minnesota

Yes International Publishers
1317 Summit Avenue, Saint Paul, MN 55105-2602
651-645-6808
www.yespublishers.com.

A Note from the Author

Welcome to Mirrors for Men. These pages invite you to self-discovery. They are set up as choices—not as "shoulds"—to give you opportunities for thinking of yourself and others in new ways.

The daily thoughts and exercises propose new ideas for fun, enrichment, new views, and testing some of your unused muscles of awareness. They aren't meant to bore you but to surprise you, to tone up your emotions, to shift your perspective on yourself and your world.

Some of the things you are asked to perform may be risky, not to your wallet, but to your feelings. But how far can you really go in life without taking a few risks? The exercises are suggestions for experiments; you decide just how far you are comfortable in taking them.

Sometimes in these pages it will be suggested that you write an affirmation on your mirror. It will inspire you and remind you of a deeper truth. You can write them on your bathroom mirror, your dressing room mirror, or another mirror that you will see at least twice daily. Writing on your mirror is easy and fun, especially when you use a water-based marker that wipes off quickly. It's your own handwriting on the mirror that counts. Seeing your words through your reflection launches that day positively. Reading your affirmations out loud boosts their momentum.

These pages are put together for you because living well is a skill that develops through practice. Our hope is that this book stretches you to develop that skill.

Justin

Think of three men you call your friends.
Write their names down where you can be reminded of them.

Reflect on these words of Aristotle:
"There is no virtue without friendship."

Tell your listed friends today that they are your friends.

Have dinner with one of your male friends this week.

Talk with at least one other male about what it means to be male.

Talk with at least one other male about what you wish for men.

Write this on your mirror: I am strong enough to be vulnerable.

Reflect on this quotation from Francis Bacon:
"If a man be gracious and courteous to strangers,
it shows he is a citizen of the world."
Are you a world citizen?

Explore a different culture.
Go to an ethnic restaurant tonight and enjoy the differences.

Go to a community ethnic event and enjoy the differences there.

View a movie from another culture.

Speak to someone from a culture different from your own today. Find your familiarities and your differences.

Read a piece of literature written by a foreign author.

Reflect: What can I do to become a world citizen?

Henry Wadsworth Longfellow wrote:
"Lives of great men all remind us
that we can make our lives sublime."
What great men have influenced your life?

Read a biography of one man from history whom you admire.

Choose a quotation from one of your favorite historical people. Write it on a card and place it where you will see it often.

Imagine sharing an evening with a favorite historical personage.
What would you ask that person?
What would you tell that person about yourself?

Think about a problem that disturbs you.
How would your favorite historical person handle it?
See the problem through the eyes of that person
and gain insight into its solution.

Tell a friend about the historical person you admire most and explain how he/she has influenced your life.

How will history evaluate you?
Write a short biography about yourself, stating your values,
beliefs, relationships as well as what you have accomplished
in your life.

Think of three fun experiences that you had with your father. Write them down as you think of them.

Today write about one valuable way that you are like your father.

Reflect: What has your father given you that you cherish?

What has your father given you that helped you to become a man?

Do something today or tomorrow that helps a younger male.

Use today for forgiveness.

*Write a letter to your father
thanking him for what you gained from knowing him.
If he is alive, mail it to him.*

Write three things that you like about yourself.

Write three things that you do not like about yourself.
Think of ways to change them.

Choose one part of yourself you wish to change.
Take an action that will begin to bring the change about.

Take a second step today!

Do something nice for yourself today because you deserve it.

Today, when you find you are putting yourself down, remember "I like myself unconditionally."

Today thank someone for what they have done for you in the past.

Organize your desk today.
Does confusion leave your life somewhere else as well?
Do you like being organized?

Write on your mirror: I have more than I need to be successful.

Declare general amnesty for all your enemies.

Two words free you from the weight and sorrow of your mistakes.
They are: love yourself.

Write on your mirror: I let go of shame.

Think at least two impossible thoughts today. Write them down.

With yourself today carry something in your pocket that symbolizes your strong self.

Write on your mirror: I am more than my successes.

Write on your mirror: I am more than my failures.

How can I nurture myself today?

Write on your mirror: I am full of light.

Explore the wonder of meeting someone new.
Go to a coffee shop, request to sit down near a stranger,
and introduce a conversation.

Take a course in a new subject.
Study cooking, art, or something you were always curious about.

Take a stroll after lunch today.

In your pocket today,
carry something that symbolizes your restful self.
Check it often.

Do something today that reaches toward your restful self.

Write this on your mirror: I trust myself so I can live fully.

Visualize your goal for the day when you just wake up.
Notice how your day goes. Different?

Tell a joke today and make someone laugh.

Write on your mirror: I am a positive person.

If you get upset today, go to a private spot
and take ten deep breaths.
Notice how your awareness changes.

Buy a model kit and put it together.
Notice how your hands are more adept than when you were a child.
Congratulate yourself and admire your work.

Invite someone on a walk or bicycle ride today.

Sit in silence for a while today and savor one of your creative ideas.

*Write about one of your creative ideas
and think how you might bring it into fruition.*

Cook a meal today and invite someone to share it with you.

Write on your mirror: I am worthy of the life I want.

What does your loved one enjoy? Learn something about it today.

What can you do to surprise your loved one today?

Today give something to a cause that you believe in.

Learn more about the cause that you believe in.

Do one thing today that is unique to this season. Then write about it.

List five things that you procrastinate about.
Why do you procrastinate?

Today do one of the things on your procrastination list.

Write this on your mirror: Worry is extra.

Introduce two of your favorite friends to each other.
Plan something for the three of you to do together.

Write a poem in your own hand
(your creation or one that captures your intent)
and send it to your mother.

Do something frivolous today with someone close to you.

Say one positive thing to each person you meet today.

Pretend you are magical! Dream a miracle for someone today.

Commit to learn something about nature today.

What are your daily rituals? Do they still serve you?
Do you need to eliminate any? Change some? Add some?

Go for a contemplative walk today.

Make a wish book. Fill it with cut out pictures of your dreams.

Name one or more women you call friends.
Write their names on the page below.

Tell your listed women friends that they are your friends and why they are important in your life.

Write this on your mirror:
I am capable of warm friendships with women.

Ask each of your women friends
to tell you one quality they like about you.

Learn a new recipe.
Make it and serve it to someone you care for.

Write on your mirror:
I am ready for whatever fortune hands me today.

*Ask each of your women friends to tell you
one quality they would like you to change.*

Write on your mirror: I manage my time well today.

Write below the name of three people you have hurt in some way.
Try to understand why it was done.

Today make amends with one of the people you have hurt.

Carry something in your pocket today
that symbolizes your spiritual self.

Sort through your sock drawer. Throw away the ones not usable.
Pair up the matches. Throw away the singles.
As a reward, buy yourself a new pair of socks.

Remember: Fortune favors the bold!

Greet people differently today. See what happens.

Smile at strangers today as you pass. Enjoy.

Write on your mirror:
I am more than all my valuable ideas.

Write on your mirror:
I am strong; I am compassionate; I am a man.

Write your goal for today.
This evening write a report about it below.

Do something extravagant today with someone close to you.

Go out and buy something special for yourself.

Write on your mirror:
I allow myself to be nurtured from within.

Ask people who are close to you
what value you hold for them outside of income.

Take a favorite child to lunch.

*Make something with your own hands
for someone you love and give it to that person.*

*Make something for yourself
that you always wanted to make but didn't take the time to do.*

Notice today how different people express their anger.

Notice today how different people express their joy.

*Write below three things that you have learned
from grief, loss, or sorrow that has made you a better person.*

*In what way would you honor your feelings of grief,
loss, or sorrow today? Is it different from the past? Why?*

Write on your mirror: I continually learn.

If it is difficult for you to express compassion to other men, imagine what words you would like to hear from a friend in your moments of grief.

Write on your mirror: I am an aware human being.

Today notice if there is a difference in the way you talk to men and to women. Does your habit serve you?

Notice what you pay attention to when you talk to people.
Is it the sound of their voice? Body parts?
Content of ideas? Your own thoughts?
As an experiment, attend to something different today.

*Today send good, caring, healing thoughts
to someone who needs them.*

Take two dissimilar ideas and ponder them awhile for unlikely associations. Be creative. Jot them down.

Take a drive by yourself.
Just let your mind wander to the beauty of nature;
let it go where it will.

Go to a quiet café with a book you've wanted to read.
Treat yourself to a favorite drink and read for an hour.

Think of three fun experiences you had with your mother.
Write them down below.

Today think of one valuable way that you are like your mother.

Use today for forgiveness of your mother.

*Write a letter to your mother
thanking her for what you gained from knowing her.
If she is alive, mail it to her.*

Today notice the body shapes
of the people you meet or pass on your way.
Marvel at the great variety
and give thanks for the shape of your own body.

Today notice the great variety of skin color in all the people
you see or pass on your way.
Marvel at the beauty of each and affirm the color of your own skin.

Write on your mirror:
My body is beautiful and serves me well.

Do something special for your body today
to affirm its beauty and uniqueness.
Have a massage, relax in a scented bath, smooth on skin lotion.
Be creative.

Reflect on this:
Do you face your future looking through a rearview mirror?

Let your description of yourself conclude: That's how I was!

Contact an old friend today.

Become an observer.
Browse through life today, noticing people and events
without judging them.

Write on your mirror: I am a strong human being.

Lose yourself for an hour in your hobby today.

Make a favorite quotation book or webfile.
Fill it with words you admire.
Write one of your favorite quotations below.

Do unto others as they would do unto themselves at their best.

Treat yourself to a massage. Enjoy the pleasure that it gives you.

Congratulate yourself on an accomplishment this day.

In your pocket today
carry something that symbolizes your deeper self.

Do something today that reaches toward your deeper self.

Play today. Buy yourself a balloon!

Write on your mirror:
The earth is alive; I am part of the earth.

Books from Yes International Publishers

Justin O'Brien, Ph.D.
>Walking with a Himalayan Master: An American's Odyssey
>Superconscious Meditation
>A Meeting of Mystic Paths: Christianity and Yoga
>The Wellness Tree: Dynamic Program Creating Optimal Wellness
>Running and Breathing
>Mirrors for Men: A Journal for Reflection

Linda Johnsen
>A Thousand Suns: Designing Your Future with Vedic Astrology
>The Living Goddess: Tradition of Mother of the Universe
>Daughters of the Goddess: Women Saints of India
>Kirtan! Chanting as a Spiritual Path (with Maggie Jacobus)

Theresa King
>The Spiral Path: Explorations in Women's Spirituality
>The Divine Mosaic: Women's Images of the Sacred Other

Phil Nuernberger, Ph.D.
>Strong and Fearless: The Quest for Personal Power
>The Warrior Sage: Life as Spirit

Swami Veda Bharati
>Subtler than the Subtle: The Upanishad of the White Horse
>The Light of Ten Thousand Suns

Prem Prakash
>Three Paths of Devotion

Ron Valle and Mary Mohs
>Opening to Dying and Grieving: A Sacred Journey

Rev. Alla Renee Bozarth
>Soulfire: Love Poems in Black and Gold

Charles Bates
>Pigs Eat Wolves: Going into Partnership with Your Dark Side

Mary Pinney Erickson and Betty Kling
>Streams from the Sacred River: Women's Spiritual Wisdom

Cheryl Wall
>Mirrors for Women: A Journal of Reflection

Gopala Krishna
>The Yogi: Portraits of Swami Vishnu-devananda

Christin Lore Weber
>Circle of Mysteries: The Women's Rosary Book

Laurie Martin
>Smile Across Your Heart: The Process of Building Self-Love